Predictive Text

"Crystal Warren has distilled the art of poetry to its rarefied essence. Her words are simple and immediately accessible, but reward multiple re-readings and long scrutiny. She contemplates the divine with the same rapt attention that she gives to the vicissitudes of children. The fear that runs like a dark thread through this collection is the dread of being silenced or unheard – a poet's fear of having her voice taken away. *Predictive Text* ensures that this fear is moot, because Warren's words will certainly live on." –**Fiona Snyckers**

Predictive
Text

Crystal Warren

Published in 2019 by Modjaji Books
Cape Town, South Africa
www.modjajibooks.co.za
© Crystal Warren
Crystal Warren has asserted her right to be
identified as the author of this work.

Edited by Arja Salafranca
Cover text and artwork by Carla Kreuser
Book layout by Andy Thesen
Set in Legacy

ISBN print: 978-1-928215-82-0
ISBN e-book: 978-1-928215-83-7

In memory of Clive Newman, whose death inspired the title poem, and Ray Warren, who died the week before the collection was accepted.

Contents

Breaking Silence

Rituals

I use words
to counter chaos.

I map the mountains,
exploring peaks and valleys,
avoiding avalanches.

I tell myself stories,
leaving pebbles on the path
so I can find my way home,
one word at a time.

And it was good

In the beginning
Silence – darkness
Then a word – light

Now the world never sleeps
Lights sparkle and dance
Words sing

Across the night
We send our words
Each letter lighting the way

To another beginning

Biblios

The libraries I have loved
have been close to churches.

A curious coincidence,
or a pattern of my passions.

Places of words – the word,
of books – the book.

Old stone buildings
protecting and nourishing

a love of words,
words of love.

Breaking silence

for John

a fellow writer on the phone
on a night when I
was feeling sad

I was glad for the call
I needed to talk to someone
but was too shy to say anything

no intense conversation
we chat about our writing
poetry and fountain pens

yet my spirits lift
comforted by a friendly voice
knowing I am not alone

Susurration

for Ingrid

"Write about susurration," she says,
a dear friend now distant
as we embark on an exchange of emails,
our own electronic writing group.

So I sit at home, pen in hand
trying to write a poem
but the word wafts away,
will not be pinned down.
The meaning whispers
in the back of my mind,
then drifts into silence.

I consult my dictionary but can't find the word there.
I turn to the thesaurus, which also disappoints.
But soon I am distracted
by the many ways to describe wind.
One entry leads to another,
following references and synonyms
I lose myself in a whirlwind of words
and that poem remains unwritten.

In quarantine

I try to write my story,
to trace the paths I took.
But I am no archivist, not much is preserved.

What am I left to say of my life?
It was the day before – when I was thirteen,
once upon a time – in the beginning ...

The past is another world, shadows
remembered in a dream – fragments,
photographs – headstones – relics.

The wall of words – a child can climb it.
We all escape – but few return.
Silence covers the past in quarantine.

Shout

shout your sermon in the street
perform your poetry for the people
throw away the microphone
let your voice be heard

if speeches are suppressed
do not be silent – sing
throw away the restraining voice
let your words be heard

Words flow

words flow from my mind
filling the page with my thoughts
my pen tracing my truth

Fragile Fairy Tales

Ashes

the fire burns slowly
smoke rises soft as a sigh
but there's no warmth
in this glow

The dream of the Minotaur

Lost in the labyrinth
I wait, I wonder.
When will my saviour come?

Who will set me free
from winding paths,
screams in the night?

There are monsters in the dark.
I hear them roar,
but they do not speak to me.

I am trapped in silence
in the maze of the heart.

I long to return
to the world of men.

Slowly I unravel.

Foolish mermaid

for the sake of a man
I forsake the safety of the sea

cut out my tongue
walk on glass

dance for your smiles
the words you will not say

slowly I fade away –
foam upon the shore

The ocean in my eyes

The sea is calm today,
more like a lake than an ocean,
but do not be deceived;
beneath the smooth surface
flows a deep current
waiting for the unwary
to be swept away
and dashed on the rocks.

Fragile fairy tales

I am realistic enough
not to hope
for happily ever after

But is it so unreasonable
to wish for
once upon a time?

Waiting for Harry

once there was a boy
who became a wizard
with magic so strong
when he cast his spell
a world was enchanted

Olive Schreiner

On an African farm
she wrote her story
the iron words
prizing open doors
taking her
across the world
to share dreams
and thoughts
on South Africa

An international success
she campaigned for peace
and personal freedom
her pen an olive branch
stronger than a sword
it tore through lies
calling for justice
for equal rights
for women and labour

She changed worlds
in dream life and real life

Patriarchy 101

Half an hour into
the Women's Day event
we have yet to hear
a woman's voice.

Predictive Text

Caller ID

for Clive

My cellphone falls silent.

I find myself
obsessively checking
just in case you called.

I flip through the phone log:
calls made, received or missed,
smses in and out.

Your name appears
again and again,
a long line of words

come to an abrupt end.

I put down the phone
which can no longer reach you
and cry your name

into the silence.

Predictive text

My cellphone
keeps changing
Clive to alive.

I would give
all I own
for it to be true.

Ash Wednesday

ash on my forehead
a sign of my suffering
a season of pain

I try to reflect
on the true meaning of Lent
to focus on God

but my mind keeps on
turning to thoughts of you
your body now ash

Every April

if you were here
I could wish you
a happy birthday

but you are gone
and I have no words
of happiness

Long Distance

Elevation

take three children
add a trampoline
expect exuberance

apply daily doses
for the duration of holiday
see spirits soar as bodies bounce

Travis on his first Christmas

Eight months old, not too sure
what all the fuss is about,
you are more excited
by the bright paper
than the presents inside.
This is just as well
as Father Christmas
brings mostly clothes,
with one token toy.

But you do enjoy the day.
There are extra people
to entertain you,
to carry you around and play.
There is excitement,
music, flashing lights
and you are loved
as much as any child
in a manger.

Epiphany

The tree is dismantled,
the decorations packed away.
The children help, reluctantly,
little left of the joy
of the reverse operation.

Another Tarzan Story

for Kira

"Tell me another story about Tarzan,"
she says. Three years old
and discovering the delights
of storytelling on demand.
At first I comply, pleased
to share the joy of words.
But after three days
I begin to fade, find
myself suggesting a video,
a swim, any distraction.
Promising one last story.
And they lived happily
ever after. The end.
With barely a pause for breath
comes the request,
"Tell me another story.
A different one about Tarzan."
And so the story starts
again and again.

Long distance

I sit in silence,
alone in my flat.
At the end of the line
my sister has another life.

Our conversation is broken
by a background chorus:
two small boys laughing,
playing, fighting, crying.

Constant asides:
Christopher be careful!
David don't do that!
Ask Daddy, I'm busy.

They demand to talk to me,
cheerful voices chirping,
echoing in my mind,
long after I put down the phone.

Home baked

Sometimes skills
skip generations,
parents who lack the patience
to teach their children.

My mother,
who loved to bake,
let us "help" her
despite our hindrance.

We played in the kitchen:
decorating gingerbread men,
cutting out biscuits
mixing batters and licking bowls.

We made a mess.
We slowed things down.
We burned biscuits
and ruined pots.

But in my mother's kitchen
we made memories.
We learned to be creative,
to taste the sweetness of life.

Not Another Love Poem

Falling

Because I always
end up falling
I watch my feet.

I walk carefully,
wear sensible shoes.
I never run.

Because I always
end up falling
I watch my heart.

I try not to care,
to tread lightly.
I never dance.

Now and again

I always fall
for unavailable men.
All my studying
and I never learn.
Now it is you.

All my lost loves,
too many to count.
At night I dream
of happy endings.
Now I dream of you.

I tell myself,
tomorrow will be different.
I will not succumb
to a stranger's smile.
Then I meet you.

And once again I fall.

Solo

I'm tired of dancing
by myself

I need your touch
to set me free

take my hands
so we can fly

Reflections

I see you and me
reflected in a mirror
standing together
deceptively close
If that was a photograph
we would look like a couple
In the mirror world
my arm is around you
But out here
we never touch

Not another love poem

I resist
writing
about you

for then
I have
to face

the facts
my pen
reveals

no matter
what words
I write

you will
never
love me

On the radio

There's a song playing
a stranger saying
the words I long to hear

How does he know
the feelings I can't show
the music in my mind?

In the cards

If you play your cards right
you might find yourself
the Queen of Hearts.

But if you get a bad hand
you could be doomed
to a long game of solitaire.

Almost touching

two coffee mugs
abandoned on a table
handles almost touching

my only evidence
that for one moment
I was not alone

Speechless

driving in your car
never going very far
the silence of your touch
when words are not enough
leaves so much left unsaid

Steps

Walk
safely my
love, each step

taking
you away
one step further

away
from me
where I wait

wishing
I could
walk with you

Tracings

in the rain
I see your smile

your laughter carries
on the wind

traces of you
entrance me

Without you

every night
a storm rages
dreams tease

tears fall
morning rain
as I awake

another day
another night
just like before

the only difference
is time

Compassion Fatigue

Ghost writing

these pictures
painted on a rock
preserved through the years
portraits of a people dead
passed into the spirit world
paper cannot capture
their power

Darkness rising

the swords gather strength
the sound of weeping grows
the drums of despair beat louder
hoofbeats thunder across the land
once more the rivers run red

the horsemen ride again

Compassion fatigue

The world watches in horror
as the earth quakes,
shattering cities, entire countries.

We weep for the dead,
follow reports of rescues,
raise funds for reconstruction.

Who would guess
how soon we would forget,
distracted by the next disaster?

Mother Nature raises her voice

earthquakes, tsunamis,
hurricanes and tornadoes,
volcanoes erupt.

just a series of
natural disasters, or,
are we in trouble?

No awakening

I have dreamed dozens
of children into life

each month I mourn
the potential person lost

now I walk to work
past the rubbish bin

where a living baby
was left to die

its cries
haunt my dreams

Black Twilight

Black twilight

bleeding in time
to the song of the moon

tides flow silently
over silver sands

dreams slowly decay
with each dying day

as the wild wolves howl
Diana weeps with me

Darkness visible

I cast no shadow
in this place.
Insubstantial,
silence surrounds me
seeping through my soul.
A strangled cry
unheard.
Uncaring
the crowd continues
on its way
without me.
What webs
connect them
and why am I
cut off?
Cast out.
Can you see me?
Do I even exist?
Or am I merely
a figment
of my own
imagination?

This endless night

I wander in the rising gloom
searching for the horizon.
If I can see the setting sun
I might believe it will rise again.
Trees do a slow dance of despair
stretching up to the
dark and empty sky.
In the distance I see a hill.
Each upward path leads me back
to this valley
these trees

this endless night.

Shadow dance

the ghosts are gathering
grouped around my bed
they grope my mind

voices call to me
crying in the night
screaming in silence

shadows grow
dark flames dancing
cold fire burning

blinding the eye
binding the inner being
breaking the boundaries

washing away the walls
beneath the borders of consciousness
the words which ward off despair

the lines I write
to hold myself together
clutching at clichés

I fall silent
my tongue strangled
tears the only touch

tearing the skin
separating me from madness
the void within

no sleep tonight

Sinking

The waves beat me down.
I struggle to rise above them
but my heart drags me down.

There is no bottom
to this sea of sadness.
The waves wash over me.

Swept away

Walking in the wind
I lift my arms,
hold them out
like a child
playing aeroplanes.

I want to fly,
to float on the wind,
to be carried away
to a sheltered place
where arms are open
waiting to catch me
when I fall.

Vertigo

The world spins.
Or is it me?
I stand still,
struggling to find
equilibrium.

But my inner ear
betrays me,
whispers words
I want to hear;
an aural illusion.

The echoes bombard.
I can't shut my ears
so close my eyes.
That grows worse as
waves of darkness
overwhelm me.

I sink to the floor,
back against the wall.
Seeking support,
something solid
to hold on to,
to convince myself
that I am not
completely unstable.

Toothless

I wake from fevered dreams,
disturbing images,
sensations so real
I rub my jaw
relieved to find
everything intact.

In the bathroom
I rinse my mouth,
half expecting
the crunch
of crushed teeth,
the taste of blood,
shards in the basin.

I wonder what it means
that I dream of my mouth
disintegrating.
I try to explore it
in my journal,
but I have no words.

Incandescent

I lie in a white room:
white roof, nearly white walls
covered with black and white photographs.
The bedding is white,
as is the door, and the blinds,
closed to keep out the light.

If I looked in the mirror
my face would be white.
But I do not look.
I close my eyes,
seeking refuge in darkness
which is seared by white lightning.

The chocolate cure

My friend phones,
commiserates on my migraine:

"I saw your post on Facebook,
thought it said heartache
and wanted to make you
a chocolate cake.
Then I saw headache
and decided it was
not a good idea."

I disagree.
Chocolate cake
is always
a good idea.

Spilt

I would not have wept
over milk
but the strawberry jam
mixed with shards of broken glass
spreading over the kitchen floor
caused a sticky sadness.

Petrichor

Soft rain at the end
of a hot, humid day.

A gentle spatter
on the umbrella.

The tar glistens
and steams

releasing the smell
of summer.

Still life

So many voices
so many words
filling every space

blocks of sound
building up
breaking down

casting the first stone
a wall of words
a wave of sound

and somewhere in the noise
and chaos, I need to find
the still small voice of calm.

Not in the thunder, wind or fire
but buried beneath:
in the absence is the essence.

I sit at the door of the cave
I have run, I have walked,
now I retreat and wait

wait for an angel to bring me bread
to send me to sleep, to rest
to wake refreshed

for the journey is too much for me.
In the barrage of sound I have lost my voice.
My tongue is trapped in silence.

Speech seems hopeless.
All I can hear is the thunder of tears
the fire of a heart in turmoil.

I need to learn to listen
to embrace the solitude
to find the silence within.

In the beginning

when I woke
for the first time

I saw your face
dark eyes shining
in the empty sky

your mouth
breathed life
into my soul

and it was good

Versions of some of these poems have appeared in the following publications:

Aerial, Carapace, Echoes, A Hudson View, Incwadi, Kotaz, New Contrast and *Stanzas*.

Experimental Writing: Africa vs Latin America, edited by Tendai Renos Mwanaka and Ricardo Felix Rodriguez. Bamenda (Cameroon): Langaa RPCIG, 2017

The Ground's Ear: Contemporary Verse from Southern Africa, edited by Frederick de Jager. Cape Town: QuickFox, 2011

Heart of Africa: Poems of Love, Loss and Longing, selected by Patricia Schonstein. Cape Town: African Sun Press, 2014

The Looking Glass Anthology: Through the Single Gal's Lens, compiled by Flow Wellington and Jowhari Trahan. Johannesburg: Poetree Publications, 2019

Poems for Haiti, edited by Amitabh Mitra. East London: Poets Printery, 2010

The Sol Plaatjie European Union Poetry Anthology; Vol III, compiled by Liesl Jobson. Johannesburg: Jacana Media, 2013

The Avbob Poetry Project – https://www.avbobpoetry.co.za/

Badilisha Poetry X-change – https://badilishapoetry.com/

About the author

Crystal Warren grew up in Port Elizabeth but has spent her entire adult life in Grahamstown/Makhanda. She has studied Librarianship, English Literature and History, and works as a librarian, literary researcher and museum curator. She edited *New Coin* poetry magazine for four years and has taught creative writing courses and workshops. Her poems have been published in several South African journals and anthologies. Her first collection of poems *Bodies of Glass* was published by Aerial Publishing in 2004.

Author photo: Zongezile Matshoba

Printed in the United States
By Bookmasters